Anthony Guggenberger

Liudolf

A historical drama of the time of Otto The Great

Anthony Guggenberger

Liudolf
A historical drama of the time of Otto The Great

ISBN/EAN: 9783741156083

Manufactured in Europe, USA, Canada, Australia, Japa

Cover: Foto ©Andreas Hilbeck / pixelio.de

Manufactured and distributed by brebook publishing software (www.brebook.com)

Anthony Guggenberger

Liudolf

LIUDOLF.

A HISTORICAL DRAMA

OF THE

TIME OF OTTO THE GREAT.

IN FIVE ACTS.

For Colleges, Young Men's Societies, Etc.

By A. GUGGENBERGER, S. J.

DRAMATIS PERSONÆ.

OTTO I, the Great,
LIUDOLF, eldest Son of Otto,
ST. ULRICH, Bishop of Augsburg,
HENRY OF BAVARIA, Otto's Brother,
CONRAD OF LORRAINE, Otto's Son-in-law,
ARNULF, Count Palatine,
HENRY, Count of Kempten,
ROLAND of Kyburg,
DIETBOLD of Dettingen, } Brothers of Ulrich,
MANGOLD,
BRUNO, Chaplain to St. Ulrich,
EBERHARD, an Officer,
RUPERT,
KUNO,
KURD, } Bavarian and Suabian Soldiers,
LOTHAR,
PHILIP,
WALDEMAR,
ECKARD, } Saxon Soldiers,
WOLFRAM,
TOCSONY, newly elected Chief of the Magyars or Hungarians,
GEYSA, his Son, later first Christian King of Hungary,

Dramatis Personæ.

LEHÉL, a Hungarian Duke or Prince, - -
FYNN-UGRIA, ⎫
OSTYAK,   ⎬ Taltos or Magyar Priests,
MAROT,   ⎭
BENNO, a Peasant, - - - - -

Boys, Pages, a Chamberlain, Messenger, Hungarian Scouts and Warriors.

LIUDOLF.

ACT I.

PALACE SCHOOL OF OTTO I. IMPERIAL PALACE OF MAINZ.

ST. ULRICH, Bishop of Augsburg, on a visit in Mainz.
PRINCE LIUDOLF, son of Otto I. BOYS. PAGES. CHAMBERLAIN. A MESSENGER.

Liudolf leans against a pillar. A page hands him a tablet. Liudolf reads excitedly; writes a few words, and puts his seal on the tablet, which he returns to the page. Page exit. During this dumb action Ulrich is speaking to the boys.

Ulrich.
Tell me, my boys, what law God's finger wrote
To head the second tablet of his code.
 First Boy.   I know!
 Second Boy.   The fourth commandment.
 Third Boy.   Honor thou
Thy father and thy mother.
 Ulrich.   Right, my child.
God's pledged reward on who obeys his
 father,

Be he the son of freeman or of serf,
Of Duke or Margrave, nay the king himself.
But woe the child that spurns his parents' will.
And who can tell me of a wicked son
Whom God's just wrath struck down in blooming age,
When he had raised his hand against his sire?

Fourth Boy.
Was it not David's son, proud Absalom?

Ulrich.
It was proud Absalom. With charioteers,
And mounted horse and runners fleet he scoured
His father's land; and sitting by his gate
He spake sweet words of cheer to all the men
Of Israel that sought the royal court.

Fifth Boy.
And was it wrong for him to lead his men,
His foot and horse in gorgeous calvalcade
And well bespeak the vassals of his sire?

Ulrich.
It was great wrong to steal from David's heart
The hearts of Israel and win them o'er
To his own soaring scheme. His spies went forth
To lure the tribes to him with loud proclaim:
"An ye shall hear the trumpets sound, say ye:
To Hebron all! There Absalom is king."

Third Boy.
O, foul betrayer of his gracious liege —
His own dear father and his royal lord.
Ulrich.
And when the rebels made for Hebron's camp,
King David hid his face and fled his son.
Fourth Boy.
Ha, had our Otto been the king betrayed,
[LIUDOLF *starts*]
He would have rallied round his Saxon hosts,
And ridden down the rebels like a swarm of
Magyar dogs.
Fifth Boy [*fiercely*].
Why, braggart, not the Franks
As well? Otto himself was made a Frank,
And crowned on Frankish soil.
Ulrich.
A truce, a truce
To this untimely strife [*aside*]; alas, a type
Of our factions, feuds, and jealousies
That rend the nation, yea, the royal house —
[*To the* BOYS.]
You know the end, the battle, the defeat,
The rebel son caught up 'twixt heav'n and earth
Within the branches of the fatal oak
And pierced with Joab's lances, — slain at last
By ten young armor-bearers of the chief.

Second Boy.
By Roland's mace, a most unknightly death.
Ulrich.
'Twas God who thus avenged the fourth command.
Liudolf [*approaching* ULRICH *excitedly*].
Had Absalom an uncle at the court
Who poisoned David's ear against the son?
Ulrich.
Hush, Liudolf, respect the sanctity
Of unsuspecting childhood. [*To the* BOYS].
   Out with ye!
Hie to the games beneath the thunder oak
You like so well. A hunting horn to him
Whose flying arrow hits the cleanest mark.
All the Boys.
Ho! to the target! ho! a prize, a prize!
Ulrich.
You've opened an abyss before my feet.
And you, my Prince, an Absalom! How oft—
Knowing the trend of your ambitious mind,
In tears and supplications did I plead
With God on high to save my Liudolf
From what his tongue has just revealed to me!
Liudolf.
My tongue, maybe, has run away with me;
I know your loyalty to — to — my sire;

My speech may smack of madness or of worse,
But you, at least, I trust, are not the man
To act the tell-tale on your former ward.
I *cannot* bear this life at Otto's court.

Ulrich.

Your *father's* court!—And why not, Liudolf?
Art thou not second in the German realm?

Liudolf.

A murrain on this fraud! Second, indeed!
Who holds the Emperor's ear? This haughty prince,
My uncle Henry, whom my father made
Duke of Bavaria; but yesterday
A rebel up in arms against the king;
To-day th' almighty counsellor of the realm.

Ulrich.

Fy, fy, my prince, the charge is undeserved.
Our noble liege, your father, as you know,
Is full as generous to who repents,
As stern and terrible to foe in arms.
True, Henry's sin was great, but greater still
His reparation. Fully did he prove
His faith upon the plains of Lombardy.

Liudolf

The plains of Lombardy? You add a sting!
Who were the first to march 'gainst Berengar
The faithless tyrant? 'Twas our Saxon youth

That filled the Alpine gorges with their songs
And clash of arms. 'Twas I that led the van.
Speak out, why were my father's cities closed
Against the son ? Because the spies and tools
Of my Bavarian uncle had the start.
Their jingling purses and their honeyed words
Unlocked with golden keys the rebel towns,
And Liudolf — but lately looked upon
As lawful heir of Europe's proudest throne,
Was left to camp in marsh and open field.
Ulrich.
Know you so little then of southern craft,
Italian cunning, as to brand your kin
With treachery of fickle Longobard ?
Shame, Liudolf, your eyes are sadly blurred,
Your mind distorted, and your judgment warped
By promptings of your pride or evil friends,
Or him whose living realm is archdeceit —
Or — could it be, that Conrad of Lorraine
Speaks with the tongue of Liudolf ? Beware!
Appointed heir of Otto's sacred crown,
The kingdom's firstborn — sainted Edith's son !
Liudolf.
You touch a tender chord — a bleeding wound
Which none but you may touch — O Editha,
King Edward's holiest child! Look down on
 me,

Liudolf.

Dear mother of my heart, true saint of heav'n!
Bring back the sinless days I lived with thee,
When thy sweet voice in league with thy sweet
  eyes
Tamed into love and peace my restless soul,
And thrilled my aching heart with holy joy.
[*Fiercely*] Ha, ha! and who holds now her
  empty place?
Who sighs and fawns at my stern father's side?
Oh! this Welsh widow — this Italian queen,
This sickly step-dame of Burgundian blood!

Ulrich.

Beware, rash youth, your speech is blasphemy!
How dare you stand before the light of God,
Such foul injustice rankling in your breast!
There is from Baltic Sound to Afric's shore
No wife so pious, gentle, pure, and true,
So self-forgetting and so generous,
So tested in the crucible of woe,
So worthy to succeed an earlier saint,
As our peerless Empress Adelheid.

Liudolf.

Let her be all you say, and ten times more!
But answer this: Who was her escort when
Her bridal train made entry through the gates
Of old Pavia? Why, my uncle Henry;
Who from the outset stole her confidence?

My uncle Henry; who advises her,
When peace or war compels his majesty
To be abroad?—my uncle evermore.
The *son* may hold his mother's sweeping train;
The *brother* guides and rules both king and queen.

[*Exter* CHAMBERLAIN:]

My Lord, excuse my haste; the urgency
Of evil news, alas, brooks no delay.
A messenger from Augsburg.

Messenger.

    Gracious liege,
The steppes of Hungary are pouring forth
Their savage hordes, the Lech on either bank
Is swarming with their bare-backed cavalry.
The heathen swear to pile the city walls,
Raised by your grace, on our devoted heads.

Ulrich.

O Lord, have mercy on my stricken flock,
And give me strength to keep the spoiler's hand
From off thy fold.— To horse, my friends, to horse!
I'll be with you, Sir Knight, a moment hence.

         [*Exeunt.*]

[*To Liudolf.*]

By all the tokens of thy noble youth,
The cherished mem'ry of thy mother's love,

The pray'rs that mount from Germany and
  Rome,
The hope of heaven and the love of God,
Halt on the brink! Th' abyss is deep and dark.
Blanche not by foul revolt thy father's hair!
Remember Absalom:— On high rules One
Who guards the Fourth Commandment. Fare
  thee well!
My suffering people calls me to my post.

Liudolf [*Alone*].

He has well-nigh unmanned thee, Liudolf!
This pure, austere, unreasonable priest.
" Appointed heir of Otto's sacred crown!"
Thus spake the bishop; but who told him so?
What knows the holy man of court intrigues?
Of signs and whisperings and secret ways
That to the watchful eye reveal the truth?
Did ever *he* observe my father's looks,
That chill my blood while his most beaming
  smiles
Fall on this infant boy of Adelheid,
Who seems to stretch his sprawling fingers
  forth
To grasp the crown once worn by Charle-
  magne?
Is this a demon, as the bishop dreams?
Distempered fancy's work? Temptation's play?
Ah, here comes light.

[*Conrad enters.*] Conrad, my noble friend,
I never needed more your calm advice.
     Conrad.
What means this clouded brow, Prince Liudolf?
     Liudolf.
I had a bout with Augsburg's bishop, faith!
I'd rather hew in twain a foeman's lance
Than face this prelate's gaze.
     Conrad.
And right thou art.
A doughty knight is he of book and cap.
A saint they call him. Little does he reck
Of guilded vanities and worldly trim.
Vile beggars eat the treasures of his see,
His retinue are widows, cripples, serfs.
At his own board he serves the vulgar herd
And wipes the fetid feet of hunchbacked churls.
     Liudolf.
But Augburg's people swear by Ulrich's name;
The Emperor reveres him as a saint,
And high and low adore the man of God.
     Conrad.
Quite natural; stoop to the mob, and lo!
The mob will throw their caps into the air.
Our Emperor is a statesman far too shrewd
To slight this champion of the cross who casts

A spell of awe upon the Magyar hordes.
Ulrich is worth an army to the king.

Liudolf.

If Conrad of Lorraine thus sounds the praise
Of Ulrich's fame, what wonder, then, if I
Feel fascinated by the prelate's power,
His holiness and his heroic speech?

Conrad.

Well, if thy princely conscience feels a qualm,
Follow at all events this saintly guide.
I will not step between thy ghostly father
And thy repentant soul. Kneel down before
This Alamannian priest and strike thy breast
And humbly own thy Saxon sins of pride.
I trow he'll not withhold from Otto's son
The boon of absolution; faith, not he!
But when you rise, foreswear, I pray, the blood
Of Widukind that courses in thy veins.

Liudolf.

And why, O mighty ruler of Lorraine,
Was Widukind debased by bowing low
To Frankish priest? At heaven's gate, I ween
Frank, Saxon, Alaman have even chance.

Conrad.

But, Prince, worse things than cringing to a
  priest
Are hanging on the issue of this hour.

What touching sight and show, Prince Liudolf
Bent on his knee, his hands in homage placed
Between the soft and plump and dimpled palms
Of baby Henry, whilst he leers enthroned,
Upon the lap of Empress Adelheid?
    Liudolf.
And why not, if I choose? The bishop spake
Of hell, temptation, sin, and foul revolt;
I'm free t' unfurl the standard of my rights,
Despite the bishop's sermon and his threats.
Friend Conrad goads me on with gibe and sneer,
And·yet I'm free to tender fealty
To Otto's brat, despite the Duke's disdain.
    Conrad.
Ah, by my soul, you go too far, my prince.
I charge you with the lie direct [*draws a tablet from his bosom*], and here
The damning proof! your word, and hand, and seal
Are duly pledged to me within this hour.
 [*Hands him the tablet*]:
"Prince Liudolf will ne'er betray his pledge."
    Liudolf.
Why, calm your silly passion, noble Duke;
You have misjudged the trend of my remarks.
Prince Liudolf will ne'er betray his pledge,

But not because he bows to outside stress,
Not even to the urging of his friend,
The Duke of Lotharingia, but because
He owes it to himself to keep his word,
E'en to his tools. If Ulrich stoops to serfs,
The Prince can well afford to stoop to Dukes.
Conrad.
To stoop — to tools — to Dukes, strong words, indeed,
I might resent the terms, but, noble Prince,
Let us not bandy words where minds agree.
When cleaving helmets is the bugle call,
I like proud fire in a princely chief.
Liudolf.
Here, then, my hand on it, we are allied
For weal or woe, thy friends shall be my friends,
Thy foes my foes.
Conrad.
Be 't so: That seals the doom
Of Henry so-called of Bavaria.
Liudolf.
The terms remain unchanged, as erst agreed,
Conrad.
The same. The ancient dukedoms are restored.
Your uncle Henry's to evacuate
Bavaria and its dependencies,
And Palsgrave Arnulf mounts the vacant seat.

Liudolf.
Conrad, my gallant ruler of Lorraine
To take possession of Franconia.
Conrad.
And Liudolf, Editha's first-born son,
To be Suabia's Duke without delay,
And in good time to wear the crown of Rome.

CURTAIN.

ACT II.

SCENE I.

Royal camp before Mainz. Knights and troopers in groups, drinking and gambling, etc.

Rupert. Ho! Bavarians, a truce to your wrangling! Here is to Arnulf!

Waldemar [*knocks the lifted goblet out of* RUPERT's *hand*]. What sayest thou, traitor?

Rupert. Well, then, to King Otto. But why a traitor? Is not the Palsgrave fighting on our side?

Waldemar. Skulking, you mean. Whenever it comes to blows he's hanging back.

Eckard. Give me King Otto, first in the fray, last at the spoils.

Waldemar. And a capital huntsman! At last he has surprised the foxes in their holes.

Kuno. And pray, who are the foxes?

Eckard. Why, you thick-skulled idiot, the two rebels over there in Mainz — the son and the son-in-law — a precious brace!

Kurd. You didn't call them foxes when you felt the lion's claws and the boar's tusks, beneath these very walls, ay, more than a dozen times in the last two months.

Walfram. Rampant enough they were. But Otto has pared the claws of the one and pulled the teeth of the other. You'll soon see them in camp, I warrant you, all down in the mouth.

Lothar. Conrad is no boar — he carries the leopard in his shield.

Wolfram. Leopard or boar, he'll soon whine at Otto's feet like the beaten cur he is.

Rupert. Curb your tongue, you Saxon hound, or I will send some of your own teeth down your garlic-scented throat.

Eberhard [an officer]. Peace there, ye impudent brawlers, or I will give you a taste of King Otto's medicine against camp-riots; you'll carry a mangy dog for three miles; good cess to you!

Kuno. Bishop Ulrich of Augsburg, too, is in camp.

Kurd, and all the Bavarians: Hurrah for the defender of Augsburg.

Saxons. Hurrah for the Hammer of the Magyars.

Kuno. Honor to whom honor is due! Methinks, the princes on either side might share the minstrels' lays.

Waldemar. 'Tis of Otto they sing: "What brave chief shall head the forces."

SAXON CHORUS.

What brave chief shall head the forces
Where the German warriors gather?
Best of horsemen, best of horses,
Highest head and highest feather.

Eckard. Otto carries the eagle in his pennant. The eagle flies highest and straightest to the sun.

Lothar. The Leopard for me! Conrad the Red forever! Best of horsemen, best of horses. Highest head and fairest feather!

Wolfram. The plague upon the traitorous liar! Wasn't Conrad beaten on the Meuse by Count Reginar, before he hid himself in this rebel nest of Mainz?

Lothar. False! Thou bragging numskull! The Leopard held his ground from noon to night; his two-hander mowed down the Flemings like withered grass, his battle axe hewed crimson avenues into their serried ranks;— night come, Count Reginar had not the brazen front you have to claim a victory.

Philip (*Suabian*). The lion has taken a spring above the eagle and the leopard. Liudolf chased Otto from Ingelheim to Mainz.
[*Enter* ROLAND OF KYBURG, *disguised as a peddler, pushing his way through the soldiers*].

The Peddler [aside].

And at Mainz he made the royal eagle pull out one of his own feathers to sign a compact which sent him skurrying down old father Rhine to Koeln.

[Aloud]. A happy day, gentlemen of the sword, one and all. Purses, rings, brushes, buckles, jewels, laces, horse-combs, gold, silver, copper, brass buttons, all as cheap as the oath of a Welsh law man.

Kuno. Begone with your litany! Give us the story of the compact of Mainz — we never heard the inside of it.

Many Voices:

The story, the story!

Peddler. You remember when Otto, our gracious King and Emperor, arrived the last time before this good city of Mainz. The Emperor fumed before the closed gates; the citizens grinned behind them. One day, however, a deputation of well-fed burghers, amidst sundry bows and scrapings, and with a peculiar twinkle in their eyes, surrendered the keys of the city into the hands of our Otto, God bless his banner! But what was his astonishment when inside he met — whom do you think he met?

Philip. Why, the Archbishop of Mainz, of whom no one knows whether he is for the father or for the son.

Peddler. False guess no guess.

Waldemar. Look out for that peddler; there's more than a peddler behind those wares.

Peddler [*aware of Waldemar — aloud*]. Bow strings, fish lines, arrow points, bills and bows — English make — fowling flutes, falcon chains, night caps — that'll settle them. False guess, no guess, as I quoth before. He met Liudolf and Conrad, face to face.

Philip. Whew! There is fire and flash for you! Steel on flint — father and son.

Peddler. Not at all, worshipful Lords. The sons were all duty, submission and filial reverence. Still, in their soft-spoken temper the dutiful sons were surrounded by an army of young war devils, whilst Otto had only a handful of sober knights and rusty squires to uphold his majesty. Thus it came about, that the honey-mouthed princes asked the venerable combination of father and father-in-law to take a quill and sign a parchment which Liudolf's pen and ink-horn man had all ready, cut and dried.

Rupert. And what, then, had the pen and ink-horn man put on that parchment?

Peddler. In the first place, No. 1, to wit: That son Liudolf should now be Duke of Suabia, and King of the Romans in the blessed time to come.

[*Flourish of trumpets on the R.; enters* HENRY OF BAVARIA *with retinue; takes his seat on a camp stool.*]

All the Saxons. Hally ho! Henry of Bavaria! Henry forever.

Kuno. Bad 'cess to the haughty favorite. And what else was contained in that parchment?

Peddler. That Conrad should be Duke of Franconia and Lorraine.

[*Flourish on the L.; enters* PALSGRAVE ARNULF *with retinue, takes seat on the left.*]

All the Bavarians. Ho! hally ho, the noble Palsgrave Arnulf! Arnulf forever!

Peddler [*in a changed manner*]: Now mind, gentlemen, the third point, and the effect it will presently produce. [*Raises his voice*].
The solemn compact signed at Mainz has placed
The ducal crown on Palsgrave Arnulf's brow,
Bavaria's hereditary Duke.

  Henry of Bavaria [*jumps up*].
Who blazes forth that treasonable writ,
Obtained by force and broken long ago

By its own perpetrators? Show your face!
Who dares to join this Palsgrave Arnulf's name
With my domain and dub the Count a Duke?
   Waldemar. That peddler there.
   Eckard. A spy! a spy!
   Henry of Bavaria. Then seize the traitor!
[*Commotion on both sides. Waldemar and Eckard try to approach the peddler; Bavarians dispute their way*].
   Kurd. [*To* PEDDLER]. Run! 'tis for your life.
   Peddler [*draws a sword from under his cloak*]. Not yet, not yet. I know and bide my time.
Arnulf.
No traitor, proud intruder, but a peer
Of gentle blood, who stands prepared to vouch
With hand and steel for right 'gainst burning wrong.
Peddler [*aside*].
Now is the time for Liudolf and Conrad
To have their say, for Arnulf's blood is up.
[*Exit*].
Henry of Bavaria.
Then see what Henry of Bavaria thinks
Of Arnulf's claims [*pulls down Arnulf's standard*

and tramples on it]. Down with the spurious rag! [*Great excitement and clash of arms on both sides; at the same time Imperial flourish* — enter OTTO I, St. ULRICH and ATTENDANTS].

Ulrich.
Down, down your swords! no naked blade must gleam
In presence of th' anointed majesty.

Otto.
What means this broil, my lords and gentlemen!
Have we to deal with vassals true and good?
Or else with brawling rival lords who place
Their petty feuds above the common weal?
What say you Palsgrave Arnulf?

Arnulf. Please, my Liege,
Some overzealous vassal stirred the bile
Of yonder Duke so-called, who in his ire
Did insolently trample in the dust,
The banner of Bavaria's ancient duke.
On hundred battlefields it showed the way
Into the heart of our country's foes
Before that Saxon Henry's worth was known.

Otto.
You dare, then, to impeach the lawful claim
Of our beloved brother, rebel bold?

Arnulf.
Rebel no worse than Henry was of late [*enter* ROLAND *of* KYBURG, THE PEDDLER, *now in knightly armor*].
May I approach your presence, gracious king,
Beneath a flag of truce, and humbly crave,
A conference for Liudolf and Conrad?
Thrown at their father's feet with sobered minds
They sue for peace and pardon.
   Otto.   Ha! They come,
When death and ruin stares them in the face,
'Tis late, forsooth, but tell the prodigals
That we shall not depart from our rule:
As their repentance proves sincere and full
Shall my forgiveness prove [*Exit* ROLAND.
  OTTO, *turning to* HENRY *and* ARNULF].
                          We'll further look
Into your quarrel once this weightier cause
Has found its settlement.
     [*Enter* LIUDOLF *and* CONRAD.]
   Liudolf.   O father, pardon!
Thy sons confess their guilt 'gainst heaven and thee
And 'gainst the common weal of our realm,
And sue for peace.
   Otto.   And who will pledge
That this new change of mind will persevere?

Conrad.
Our oath made into Bishop Ulrich's hand,
Our castles handed over to your will,
The Castellans your pleasure may appoint.

Otto.
Fair terms, indeed, if as sincere as fair.
But past experience shows your fairest terms
Compelled in days of gloom and hope dashed down,
Flung to the winds in days of hope revived.
I want a stronger proof than fickle words.
Name me the backers of this new revolt,
Your secret instigators still at large.

Liudolf.
Father, forbear, forbear to tempt your son!
The keys of Mainz, our forces, ourselves,
Take them, but to betray our absent friends,
Impossible! [*Rises.*]
My liberty is yours, my honor mine.

Otto.
And what says Conrad to this high resolve?

Conrad [*rising*].
I spurn to hand to this Bavarian Duke
A single hair of friend or follower!
'Tis he [*pointing to Henry of Bavaria*] who mars the peace and stirs this feud.

Liudolf.
'Gainst him it is, and not against yourself,
Dear father mine, that our hapless arms
Were raised in vain. Remove him from his post
And peace will reign all over Germany.
Henry of Bavaria.
And there you lie! 'Tis you who cannot wait
Till our princes seal your royal claims.
I have no power but received from him
Who is your king and mine. If I'm the man
To answer for the evils of the time,
Why roam ye burning up and down the land?
Why not assail the real criminal?
Why, foolish boy, poor tool of scheming men —
Come forward, I am ready for your blows.
Kuno.
Let Henry keep his peace! Let Ulrich speak!
Bavarians.
Ulrich of Augsburg, be our spokesman! Hear!
Ulrich.
Oh, erst our joy and now our saddest grief,
Oh, Liudolf, behold your father's head
Turned gray before its time, and you the cause.
God's blessing or God's curse lie in your hand.
Obedience or revolt will make or mar
Your destiny. God's Fourth Command will
  stand.

Down, down upon your knees and name the
  men.
Deliver them, not to revengeful fate,
But to a father's generosity.
You, once embraced within your father's arms,
Fear nothing for your friends; I pledge my troth.
     Otto.
Well, Liudolf, you hear your teacher's words,
They have my countenance. What shall it be?
  Liudolf [*silent, sullen, wavering*].
In all concerning me I will submit,
As to the rest, I stand by my resolve.
     Conrad.
And I'll uphold the prince in life and death.
  Otto.   [HENRY *whispers to Otto.*]
Is this thy last avowal?
 Liudolf. It is my last.
     Otto.
Then justice take its course, e'en 'gainst my
  son.
I solemnly proclaim the Empire's ban
Upon my guilty son and son-in-law.
May God on high decide the cause of right.
I charge you, Palsgrave Arnulf, by your oath
To apprehend the rebels; do your task!
     Arnulf.
And I refuse thy charge as instigated

By Henry so-called of Bavaria. [*Turning to* HENRY OF B.*.*].
I claim thy duchy by an earlier right.
Here is my gage. [*Throws down the gauntlet before* HENRY.]
Vassals, around your liege,
And follow me to Ratisbon.

   Henry of Kempten.   False Duke!
I, Henry, Count of Kempten, do defy thee,
And follow Arnulf.

   Knights. And so do I — and I — so do we all.

[*Meanwhile Otto and Ulrich have restrained the Saxons.*]

               Waldemar.
O, let us follow them and cut them down!

               Otto.
Stay, I command, no useless bloodshed now;
'Twould be but wanton folly. Bide your time.

   St. Ulrich [*with uplifted arms*].
Lord God of heaven, in deep humility,
Do I adore thy ways and bless the hand
That strikes us for our sins. With trembling awe
And fervent thanks I hail the coming day
When Thou, the King of kings, shalt vindicate
The Fourth Commandment with thy conquering
   arm.

         CURTAIN.

ACT II.

SCENE II.

A Forest. (Enter on each side a Hungarian scout, they lie flat on the ground and listen.)

First scout [rising]. No foot-fall of Christian dog. No tramp of the terror-priest.

Second scout [rising]. No thud of Saxon horse-hoof — May Isten strike Ulrich with the fork of his lightning.

[*Both whistle, Enter* FYNN-UGRIA, OSTYAK *and* MAROT, *Taltos or heathen priests, with attendants*].

Fynn-Ugria. Here build Isten's altar.

Ostyak. Here strike the sacred fire.

Marot. Here immolate the hearts of Isten's three white horses.

[*Whilst the attendants build the alter the princes or dukes enter, followed by Hungarians.*]

Tocsony. Geysa, son of Tocsony, the son of Zoltan, the son of great Arpad, the son of ancient Almos, wilt thou enter to-day the ranks of free Magyars by sacrificing the hearts of Isten's three horses to Isten?

Geysa. Father mine, descendant of Great Arpad, proudly will I enter the ranks of the invincible Magyar, by striking my first blow on

Saxon crest or mail, by dipping my first arrow in Teuton blood, but not by burning horses' hearts on Isten's altar.

Tocsony. And does the son of Marot's fair daughter not believe in Isten, the Magyar God of victory?

Geysa. Geysa believes in the great ruler of the earth and the sea and the sky, whom his father and his mother, and his brothers and his sisters, and his people call Isten the Great.

Tocsony. And why, then, wilt thou not sacrifice to him?

Geysa. To sacrifice is the work of priests, to fight the call of a Magyar prince.

Tocsony. My son Geysa uses evasive words. Before fighting the Magyar prince offers his sacrifice.

Geysa. Sacrifices of slain horses I will offer none.

Tocsony. What strange and untoward fancy has seized my Geysa's spirit? You speak in riddles.

Geysa. And riddle let it remain. It is a riddle to myself.

Tocsony. Speak out, Geysa, I command. There is more in your fancy than a riddle — there is a secret. And the son ought to have no secret unknown to his father.

Geysa [*after a thoughtful pause*]. "The son ought to have no secret unknown to his father." That word is true as Isten's own spirit. Hear then. When we broke into the Alamannian lands, and brought destruction to our yellow-haired foes, I wandered in deep thought one day through a lonely forest. And I chanced upon a hut built of rough timber, before which sat a — a —

Tocsony. Whom didst thou meet in the silent woods?

Geysa. How shall I tell thee! He was a man clad in a brown coarse garment falling to his feet — nay, he was a spirit in the guise of man. In his eyes, heaven's purest blue, light's most brilliant ray — nay, something fairer than sky and light, fair beyond anything in the steppes of Buddha or in the waves of the Danube or in the morning star. My soul was moved within me. He spoke to me of Isten. He spoke to me as no priest ever spoke. Alas, I could not retain his words, they were too overpowering, too sweet, too fleeting to be more than lightning flashes in the midnight darkness of my mind. But one thing he asked of me, one thing I promised him — never to sacrifice aught on earth to Isten but the pure thoughts of my soul. And, father mine, I must keep my promise.

Tocsony. And he spoke to thee of Isten?

Geysa. He spoke to me of the great and holy spirit that made the earth, and the sea, and the sky, and the soul of Geysa. He spoke to me of Isten.

Tocsony. A most mysterious tale — and true, for it is told by my son.

Geysa. Father, it is true.

Tocsony. And wilt thou, then, postpone entering the ranks of the free Magyars?

Geysa. If my father likes the word postpone I will postpone it.

Tocsony. Then I must apprise our priests, perhaps allay their suspicions and resentment. [*To the priests.*] Taltos of great Isten, perform your rites, my son is as yet unprepared for Isten's sacrifice.

[*The priests after significant looks and gestures at Geysa, place the three hearts on the fire.*]

Fynn-Ugria [*in the center*].

O thou, God, living above, great Isten,
Who hast clad the earth with grass,
Who hast given leaves to the tree,
Who hast provided the calves with flesh,
Who didst bring forth hair on the head,

RECITATIVE.

Thou creator of all created things,
Thou preparer of all that is prepared.

Ostyak and Marot [in recitative melody].
Thou creator of all created things,
Thou preparer of all that is prepared.
All. Thou creator of all created things,
    Thou preparer of all that is prepared.
Fynn-Ugria.
O listen, thou creator of the stars.
O Alton Pi, who hast created the father.
O Ulgen Pi, who hast created the mother.
{ Thou creator of all created things,
{ Thou preparer of all that is prepared.
[Repeated as above].
Fynn-Ugria.
O give us battles, O Isten,
Give food, O Isten,
Give battles to our chief, O Isten,
Give victory to our battles, O Isten.
Give thy blessing, O Kudai, O Isten.
{ Thou creator of all things created,
{ Thou preparer of all that is prepared.
[Repeated as above].
Marot. I see in the heart of the first white horse divisions in the clans of the Saxons and Boyars and Franks, and battle-fields, and murders and graves.
All. O Isten, give us a chief.
    And to the chief triumphs,
    And spoils to the Magyars.

Ostyak. I see in the heart of the second white horse the sons of the king, lifting their swords against their father and king, the great chief of the Saxons.

All. Isten, give us a chief—and to the chief triumphs, and spoils to the Magyars.

Fynn-Ugria. I see in the heart of the third white horse Magyars fighting with the sons of the king, and I see — I see — a king from the loins of Arpad — and on his crown — woe is me, woe is me!

Several dukes and Magyars. What see you on his crown, speak out O, Taltos of Isten!

Fynn-Ugria. The cross and the crucified man [*falls down in convulsions*].

Ostyak.
The fiends of Omurah must have charmed his eyes.

Fynn-Ugria [*shakes himself free and hisses in Ostyak's ear*]. Or Geysa, the infected son of Tocsony. [*Signals are heard from a distance.*]

Tocsony. Off, Magyars, to the hidden cave of Kudai. [*Exeunt destroying the vestiges of the sacrifice.*]

[*Flourish of trumpets approaching. Enter* LIUDOLF, CONRAD, ARNULF, ROLAND, *and retinue*].

Roland.
Well, well, my noble lords, in me you see
The champion peddler of all Christendom.
My box is empty like a scrivener's pate.
Instead of gathering coins I fling them forth,
And in broad daylight tell the sober truth;
Three things no other peddler dared to do,
And yet for you I got a ducal crown,
For Liudolf and Conrad an ally.

Liudolf. You played your part with consummate address.

Conrad.
Had you not won your fame in good Lorraine,
The walls of Mainz would be your monument.

Arnulf.
And next you ought to try a chaplaincy
In Ulrich's household; why, what stare you so?

Roland.
See here, this glen has seen some earlier
 guests,
The grass has not yet risen from the tramp
Of horse and man. There was a fire here.
Within this hour.
[OUTSIDE.] A prize! halloh, a prize!
[RUPERT, KUNO, and KURD *bring in* DUKE
 LEHEL].
Why, by my soul, a real Magyar prince.

Liudolf.

Conrad.
And Magyars travel not alone. From where
This straggler was picked up, a nest of them
Cannot be far. What shall we do with him?
Arnulf.
Were Ulrich here, he might besprinkle him
To save his heathen soul. But now, I fear,
He'll have to go unchristened, for from us
He'd hardly relish any ghostly help.
Roland.
Slow, noble lord, and let me try my hand
To turn this heathen prince to better ways.
What say you to engaging on our side
These swarthy warriors?
Conrad. I dislike the scheme;
It will degrade our cause beyond repair.
Arnulf.
Not so, my noble Duke. The rumor goes
That Henry of Bavaria has called in
These Magyar hordes.
Liudolf. I heard it as the truth,
That but for uncle Henry's secret aid
And wily promptings, not a Magyar foot
Would press the German soil. Have we, then, not
An equal right? The plan is excellent.
Conrad.
Act as you like, but be the outcome yours.

Roland.
Then will I parley with this Magyar prince.
I know their ways. [*To Lehel.*] How many
are you here?
Where are your tribesmen? Nay, my friend,
Try not to steal a march upon a seer!
'Tis labor lost. Rich booty will be yours,
Peace and alliance with my masters — *or* —
    Lehel.   Who are your masters?
    Roland.   Royal Liudolf,
Conrad and Arnulf, mighty princes they,
You know their territories.
    Lehel [*aside.*] 'Tis Isten points the way —
"The sons of the king,"
                [*To Roland.*]
You said alliance, *or*, what means your or?
                Roland.
A grave on German soil for all your men.
                Lehel.
Ha! ha! bold words, but empty, Teuton chief!
                Roland.
They're bold and true, my friend, and here
the proof.
These Magyar princes, priests, and leading men
Convened to sacrifice and choose a chief,
Are now concealed in what your nation calls
The cave of Kudai.

[*Lehel, staggering back.*] This is a Wizard's ken!

Roland.
Knight, peddler, seer, beggar, diplomat,
Or wizard, never mind! A word of mine,
A bugle call will send a German host
Upon the track of all the noblest blood
That sprung from Arpad's loins. What shall it be?

Lehel [*aside*].
"I see in the heart of the third white horse
    Magyars fighting
    With the sons of the King;
    'Tis the finger of Isten!
[*To Roland.*] Alliance.

Roland.
All well so far. And what your binding pledge?

Lehel [*bares his arm*].
The Magyar blood test of the covenant.

Roland. Enough!
I know your pledge and trust its binding force.
I see you carry Arpad's battle horn.
Sound on your ivory the Princes' call [*sounds a bugle call*]!
Now off and meet your tribesmen and agree
  upon the terms. [*Exit Lehel.*]
[*To the prince.*]   The matter is arranged.

I pledge my knightly honor, nay, my life
Upon the firm cohesion of the pact
This running year.   The pledge their living
  blood.   [*Enter* HUNGARIANS *led by* LEHEL.]
  Roland.   Have you resolved to act as our
friends?
  Lehel.   We have.
  Roland.   Upon what force may we rely?
  Lehel.   We are the van of 30,000 horse.
  Roland.   Your route?
  Lehel.   Through Germany to northern
    France,
And back through Italy.
  Roland.   You'll not assail
The friends of Arnulf in Bavaria,
The friends of Liudolf in Suabia
Nor Conrad's in Lorraine?
  Lehel.   We never will.
  Roland.   Well, then, we grant you passage
    and free hand
Against our foes, and guides and subsidies
To Augsburg town.   Ye princes, warriors,
    priests.
Shall these conditions be our covenant?
  Magyars.   Hooy, hooy Magyar!
  Roland.   Then let the covenant of blood
proceed.
  Magyars: Hooy, hooy Magyars!

Roland [to Tocsony]. Who is the chief to represent your race?

Lehel [baring his right arm].
I'm ready, yellow hairs. Who stands for you?
The three princes waver, finally Arnulf steps forward.

Arnulf. Down, superstitious fears! I am the man.

[*Bares his right arm.* LEHEL *draws a long, narrow dagger from his horn and opens a vein. So does* ARNULF. OSTYAK *catches the blood of both in a goblet.* LEHEL *drinks first, then* ARNULF. *During the ceremony*]:

RECITATIVE of *Fynn-Ugria.*
The arm and the sword of the Magyar
We pledge to the stranger by Isten,
The creator of all things created,
The preparer of all that is prepared.

Tocsony.
And now, to horse, to horse! Make ready, chiefs,
To join our cavalry within three hours.

[*Exeunt.*]

Liudolf.
For us the time of parting, too, has come;
To gather reinforcements different routes
Must take us on to Augsburg. Where, my lords,
Shall be our meeting-place?

Arnulf.
St. Sinbert's shrine beyond the city wall.
Conrad.
St. Sinbert's shrine beyond the city wall,
Liudolf.
Ay, ay, St. Sinbert's shrine beyond the wall.
[*Exeunt.*]
A SHORT PLAINTIVE INTERLUDE.
Geysa [*enters in deep thought*].
How long, O Isten, yet this weary search!
When shall my eyes once more behold the One,
Or man or spirit pure, who spoke of thee?
When shall his fiery word dispel the mist
Involving still my soul that yearns for light?
[*A pause.*]
Full well I feel the fever of my race
Athirst for war and blood, and yet beyond
Mere gathering spoils and burning towns amain
And slaughtering foes must be another life.
What is it? Where to find? My eyes grow dim
With ever seeking thee, mysterious life,
And never finding— peace, a moment's rest.
[*Falls into sleep.*]
[*Enter* FYNN-UGRIA *and* LEHEL.]
Fynn-Ugria.
Tocsony, Arpad's grandson, is now chief,

And he [*points to sleeping Geysa*] his tainted offspring, coming heir.

Lehel.

Look sharp, Fynn-Ugria, for woe to thee
If thou misteach — was then this boy the one
Thou didst behold in Isten's third white horse?
Fynn-Ugria.   The same, the same.

Lehel.

[*Pointing to Geysa.*]   He wore the charmed crown,
And on the crown the cross.
Fynn-Ugria.   He wore the cross.
Lehel.   Then he must die.
Fynn-Ugria.   He must; I told you so.

[*Approach the* BOY. LEHEL *draws his dagger from his horn, meanwhile* ULRICH *and* ATTENDANTS *enter on the opposite side.* ULRICH *points out the would-be murderer to his brother.*]

DIETBOLD OF DETTINGEN [*rushes forward, strikes* LEHEL's *dagger from his hands.*]   Fair play, you wretch —
Shame, shame to strike a boy, and from behind.

[LEHEL *snatches up his dagger and flees with Fynn-Ugria. Meanwhile* GEYSA *had sprung up seeing nothing but* ULRICH.]

Geysa.
Ah! Ah! My teacher of the Suabian weald.
Ulrich.
O Geysa! child of many a prayer and fast,
My prince, my prisoner, and now my son;
For I have saved thy life. I thank thee, Lord,
I thank thee for this unexpected hour.
I came to seek my wayward Liudolf—
And lo! I found my Geysa, sent by God.

CURTAIN.

ACT III.

SCENE I.

The room of ST. ULRICH, at Augsburg, Ulrich kneeling in silent prayer, Geysa looks in and around through the window, from the outside, then jumps into the room.

Ulrich.
O Geysa, restless boy, how came you here?
Geysa.
I climbed the ivy-mantled turret wall
And by these branches swung myself to you.
Ulrich.
Always the desert roamer unrestrained,
But why not heed your teacher's private hours?
Geysa.
Out on the rolling steppes of Hungary
We're free like birds. I used my native right.
Besides, you gave me leave to come and go
If I but stayed within the city walls.
My mind is torn in twain and you alone
Can heal the rift. Now tell me openly,
If your great God should make me His, must I
Forgive my mortal foes?
   Ulrich. You must forgive.
   Geysa.   [*Walking up and down.*]
Thy voice is gentle but thy teaching hard.

Think well on it. Must Geysa, then, forgive?
That bad Lehel and worse Fynn-Ugria?
Lehel, whose dagger thirsted for my blood?
 Ulrich. You must forgive them, child!
 Geysa. [*Walking up and down.*] Impossible.
Well, tell me, teacher of the silent wold,
If your own mortal enemy would slay
Before your eyes, say brother Dietbold, him
You love so well, would you forgive the deed?
     Ulrich.
At once would I forgive, an help me God.
     Geysa.
It seems beyond man's power — even yours.
     Ulrich.
Nay, child, it would be duty's simple call,
An act commanded, infinitely low'r
Than He (*points to the crucifix*) has done for
 thee and me.
 Geys .   To quench
The fire of rage before the murdered corpse
And kiss the murderer — a greater deed
Than such forgiveness seems to pass our
 strength.
     Ulrich.
Then listen. Geysa, dost thou love thy father?
 Geysa. I love him well.
I never disobeyed him in my life.

Ulrich.
And round this sacred spot in thy young heart,
Where nature's fourth commandment reigns supreme
God's graces have been hovering all this while
I humbly think. Of this, however, anon.
And now suppose your father had received
A mortal insult from some brutal slave.
The axe of justice hangs above his head,
When lo, my Geysa rushes to the block,
His heart inflamed with mercy's purest love,
And for the slave lays down his head and life
Beneath the axe, and by his written will,
Sealed with his blood, appoints the rescued slave
Heir to his wealth and brother to his heart.

Geysa.
O Ulrich, Taltos of the Christian name,
No *man* can do this deed — nor Geysa can,
Nor *Isten*, as the Magyar knows his God.
'Twould need a greater one. Perhaps *your* God
Descending from the sky might do the deed!

Ulrich.
Thy clear and open though untutored mind,
Has grasped the central truth of our faith.
Christ Jesus did still more for thee and me,
And Jesus Christ is God.

Geysa. A streak of light!
At length a hopeful ray from unseen worlds.
How was it done?
　Ulrich. We were th' offending slaves.
Man made by God, his vassal and his bond,
Rebelled against his Lord. The son of God
To stay his father's arm uplift to strike
Came down and in the virgin's womb assumed
Our human flesh. In his humanity
He suffered stripes and mockery and death,
Became the crucified and thus appeased
His father's righteous wrath and made us heirs,
Nay, brothers, in his everlasting realm.
　　　[*Enter* BRUNO THE CHAPLAIN.]
Your brothers wish to make their morning call.
　　　[*Enter* DIETBOLD *and* MANGOLD.]
　　　　Ulrich.
They're always welcome [*to* BRUNO]:
You stay with me [*to* GEYSA]: and thou to thy lookout
And scan the country from St. Martin's tow'r.
　　　　　　[*Exit* GEYSA.]
What, Dietbold, are the tidings of this morn?
　　　　Dietbold.
I fear me, brother, there is trouble brewing
In Augsburg's neighborhood. A peasant saw
A Magyar fire-place in Hiltine wood.

Mangold.
The Magyars cannot be a numerous force.
My scouts reported no marauding hosts.
What I dread more is Arnulf swooping down
Upon our walls. Bavarian troops were seen
Around St. Sinbert's shrine.
Dietbold.
I little fear
For our good town since brother Ulrich saved
St. Afra's church from ruinous decay,
Restored the minster to its ancient grace,
And girded them and all this ancient burgh
With new and formidable towers and walls,
And more, behind these walls and towers beat
True hearts of steel, prepared to die for you.
Ulrich.
Not human arms nor granite parapets,
But God's protection is our tow'r of strength.
Dietbold.
Well, under God's protection it behooves
To wisely use our human means and strength.
Ulrich.
You're right in this, and fully I intrust
Unto my gallant brothers' watchful care
My town and flock.
Mangold.
We keep a sharp lookout;

Our trusty vassals man the battlements;
Our loyal burghers hold the armories
And guard the city gates by day and night.
   [*Enter* PAGE.]
A messenger arrived on dripping horse. [*Exit*
 PAGE.]
   [BENNO *enters.*]
God bless thee, honest Benno; whence thy ride,
And what thy tidings?
   Benno.
Well, and please, my lord,
Just ridden post-haste from St. Sinbert's shrine.
Count Arnulf's force is marching hitherward.
His plan is in the dead of night to storm
The western terrace and St. Martin's Tower.
 Dietbold. How came you by these news?
   Benno.
      I met perchance
One of his troopers, erst a chum of mine,
Who o'er a flask of Rhenish let the cat
Out of the bag. I took at once to horse.
   Mangold.
Are Liudolf and Conrad with the Count?
   Benno.
Liudolf is yet a day's march in the rear.
Of Conrad rumor says, in sulky mood
He sent his troopers home. This is all my
 news.

Ulrich.
Hast done good service, Benno, now retire;
The steward knows his task.
[*Enter* PAGE.]
Excuse, my lord,
Two Magyar envoys ask to be admitted.
Dietbold.
What? Magyar envoys? Did you hear aright?
Whoever knew of Magyar embassies
But smoking towns and fields and fleeing folk?
Ulrich.
God's sun is shining over them and us.
Christ sent his messengers to black and white,
Heathen and Jew.   Admit th' ambassadors.
[*Exit* PAGE.]
Mangold.
Nay, nay, most reverend brother, this is rash;
Shall they spy out our walls and battlements?
Ulrich.
Myself shall show them our strongest works,
The corner-stone of our citadel.
[*Enter* PAGE *with two* MAGYARS.]
First Magyar.
We come, great Taltos, from the Magyar chief;
These are his words: Give up this very hour
Young Geysa, son of Tocsony, or else [ULRICH
whispers to CHAPLAIN, *who leaves the room*].

His sword will eat thy people and his torch
Devour thy vineyards, fields, and villages.
    Dietbold [*drawing*].
May I not stop this braggart's insolence?
     Ulrich.
Peace, peace, my brother; though their words be rude
They stand protected by the nation's law.
  [*Enter* GEYSA *with* CHAPLAIN.]
These countrymen of thine demand that I
Should send thee to thy sire. What sayest thou?
    Geysa [*to* ULRICH].
I doubt me if they are my father's friends.
[*To Envoys*]. Who sent you here?
    Second Envoy.
Tocsony, Arpad's blood.
     Geysa.
You have, no doubt, a token or a sign
To vouch for what you tell me, from your chief —
For thus it was arranged 'twixt him and me.
    First Magyar.
We have — forgotten.
    Second Magyar.
We have — lost the sign.
     Geysa.
What was the sign?

First Magyar.
It was — a — silver dart.
Geysa.
Nay, my friend,
It was to be my father's topaz ring.
[*To* ULRICH]. Their message is a trap.
Because their chief
Knows and consents to my abode with you.
[*To* MAGYARS.] You're Envoys of Fynn-Ugria and Lehel.
You came to terminate the bloody work
Their steel has left unfinished, thanks to him [*points to* ULRICH].

Dietbold.
No envoys then? A wicked masquerade?
Down with the rogues, down to the lowest keep!
And let them taste the fruit of their deceit.

First Magyar.
Lay not your hands upon us, for we bear
A sign which even a degenerate
Of our race will not mistake. See here!
[*Shows sign.*]

Geysa.
'Tis true, 'tis true. 'Tis from the Khan himself.

Second Magyar.
Know by this token that a sable cloud

Of horse and men, one hundred thousand
  manes,
Is rolling hither from the Danube banks.
> ### Ulrich.
Vaunt not thy horse and men and chariots.
Your numbers may be like the ocean's sands,
There's one who holds you in his hollow hand.
Look down at my defense! [*Leads them to the
window.*] What do you see?
> ### First Magyar.
Ah! why this mockery? a freckled mob
Of beggars, cripples, sick and tottering men
And palsied women folks.
> *Ulrich.* They are my strength.

These trembling hands, these pale and palsied
  frames,
These tottering feet, my scoffing friends, will win
A triumph that all Christendom shall hail
As our holy God's own victory.
These are my champions, the poor of Christ.
Brothers, conduct these strangers to the gates.
> ### Dietbold.
And make good haste, my men, for else you
  risk
Your heads, an you are found an hour hence
Within the hearing of the curfew bell.

> [*Exeunt.*]

Ulrich.

Good Bruno, have the bells ring out and call
My flock, the rich and poor, to Afra's Church
To pray for Augsburg and for Christendom.

[*Exeunt.*]

Geysa [*alone*].

My foes are on the scent and weariless;
They thirst my blood, and hate, I fear me much,
My father for my sake; and yet I'm told,
I must forgive, forgive in duty plain.
My heart and blood cry out: No! hate for hate,
And blood for blood. And yet a whisper says:
His is the better way, *his* God forgave.
Would HE forgive, if some relentless hand
Would smite before his eyes with dagger's edge
His brother's life? I cannot think the thought,
More light, O Isten — if thou be — more light!

CURTAIN.

ACT III.

SCENE II.

The terrace and tower of St. Martin. Darkness. Stage empty. Arnulf first appears through the trap-door which is concealed behind a battlement. On the L. turrets and walls; on the R. a forest. Troopers climbing up on ladders which they subsequently pull up and place against the walls or turrets on the L. Magyars gliding in from the R., all in silence. The conversation carried on in a low voice. Arnulf, Eberhard, Lehel, Arnulf's men, Magyars.

Arnulf [*To the men climbing up*].
Take heed, th' ascent is steep — They hear us not
The terrace and St. Martin's tower are
Unguarded still — 'twill be child's play to mount
The turret, and once there the city's ours.
     Eberhard.
This storming of the best defended town
Is little short of madness — is a crime.
It is not yet too late to order back
Our army and allies.
 Arnulf.   Address yourself
To cowards, not to me. Arnulf intends
To act!

Eberhard.
But why not wait for Liudolf's
And Conrad's forces, as agreed upon
Near Kudai's grotto?
Arnulf.   Why, short-sighted fool,
Shall we divide the glory with the rest,
[*To the scalers*] Be wary there! [*to* EBERHARD]
which we can win alone?
And Liudolf, who in his inmost heart
Dotes on the bishop and his solemn ways,
Might be a dangerous marplot. And the Duke,
He never stops to mutter and to frown
At this alliance with our Magyar friends.
First break this Augsburg, Otto's staunchest fort,
And Liudolf and Conrad must accept
The fact accomplished [*superintends the scaling*].
Eberhard.
Faith, I frankly owe
I've little stomach for this bloody work.
No holier man than Ulrich in the land.
And then, this heathen bond, this Magyar crowd,
I wish them at the bottom of the sea.
Arnulf.
Our men are nearly up, the merry dance
May soon begin.

Lehel [*approaches* ARNULF].
Chief Arnulf, mind your pact:
Young Geysa, bishop Ulrich's stolen ward,
Must be my prize, not yours.
  Arnulf.   With all my heart.
Just try to bag your game! No jealousy!
[*A light appears above and the singing of "Kyrie Eleison" is heard*].
  Arnulf [*shouting*].
Up with the ladders! [SOLDIERS *shout*] Bavaria and Arnulf.
[*Magyars shout*]: Hooy, hooy, Magyar.
  Arnulf.
Quick, boys, and wing your shafts and let them fly!
Give them a volley there, a bellyful.
Here, Boyars, hug the outer barbican!
Swarm up, my men, swarm up the turret walls!
[*Above:* Kyrie Eleison. *The soldiers swarm up the ladders but are repulsed from above.*]
  Conrad.
Hungarians, out with your javelins!
Clear me those battlements.
[*Sallyport opens below, a bright light from the inside, and shouting of defenders.*]
  St. Afra and Ulrich of Augsburg!

Arnulf.
Ten thousand fiends! our plans betrayed, betrayed!
Strike for your life!
Lehel.
No fighting here for Magyars, break your ranks! [*Exeunt Magyars.*]
Eberhard.
No chance to win this fight.
Perched on this height and hung twixt heaven and earth. [*Flees with others.*]
Arnulf.
For shame, ye arrant knaves; Bavaria!
[*Meanwhile the defenders have come forward.* ARNULF *fights with* DIETBOLD *and kills him.*]
Arnulf.
There goes a gallant youth, and past repair.
Mangold.
Stand, rebel, stand!
Arnulf. Another of the brood;
The holy man has champions to spare.
Take this — and this.
[*Fighting,* ARNULF *mortally wounded.*]
The night has come forever.
[*A short pause; a few strains of funeral music. A procession of clergy with lanterns, headed by Ulrich, issues forth.*]

Ulrich.

Hie ye, my brethren, to your priestly work.

Mangold [by the shine of a lantern discovers the body of his brother.]

O Dietbold, brother Dietbold, woe is me,
Is this the issue of our hope and love?

Ulrich.

[*Followed and closely observed by* GEYSA.]

The Lord hath given him — The Lord be praised
Who took him to himself.

[ARNULF *groans in the foreground.*]

Thy soul was pure,
Thy gentle youth and life a harbinger
Of sterling worth.   Thy noble sacrifice
Went for a holy cause.   Eternal rest!
Go, bear his body to St. Afra's shrine.

ARNULF [*groaning*].

Now to that dying man.   What! is it thou!
Poor Arnulf, overtaken in thy strength.

Arnulf [turns away his head].

Ulrich himself of all the priests on earth!

Ulrich.

Leave me alone.

[ATTENDANTS *retreat, only* GEYSA *closely observes the scene.*]

My brother, I am here
To guarantee God's mercy to thy soul.

Arnulf.
Begone, thou mocking priest, no grace for me!
Ulrich.
Not so, his mercy knows as little bounds
As does the blood of Christ.
Arnulf. The blood of Christ:
In seas of Christian blood
I drowned my fealty to king and God.
Ulrich.
Lose not thy hope. Good Friday saw transferred.
A rebel from the cross to paradise.
Arnulf.
Avaunt thy lies! 'Twas I who stirred the sons
Against their father. Ay my Christened blood
Was mixed with Magyar blood in heathen rite.
Ulrich.
One sigh of penance and one tear of grief
Will cleanse thy soul from even darker deeds.
Arnulf [staring around].
I see the slain at Mainz and Ratisbon
Strong Christian men struck down by pagan darts
I hear the peasant's curse, the widow's wail,
The orphan's cry: Arnulf, false perjured knight,
Despair and die!

Ulrich. Yet stronger than all sin,
A single whispered word will shrive thy soul.
[*Wipes the blood from* ARNULF'S *face.*]
Arnulf.
Don't touch that blood, it is thy brother's blood.
Ulrich.
Nay, if thou took my brother from my arms,
Then give him back to me! I will accept
Thy precious soul, my son, as full ruturn.
Say but: Lord God have mercy on my soul!
Arnulf [*turn towards him.*]
What, Ulrich, man of God,
Dost not despair of me? not spurn and curse
The slayer of thy kin? Then there is hope.
My God, my God, I do repent my sins —
Mother of mercy, pray for fallen Arnulf.
[*Absolution.*]
Forgiveness — Otto — Conrad — Liudolf
Farewell — O holy bishop — Mary! — Christ!
[*Dies.*]
Ulrich.
Another soul snatched from the jaws of hell.
To God and to his mother be the praise.
[*Rising*].
My friends, convey him to St. Sinbert's shrine
Beyond the wall. [*Exeunt.*]

Liudolf.

  Geysa [*steps forward*].
He's stood the test; he's kept his solemn word,
He HAS forgiv'n his brother's murderer.
O Ulrich! Ulrich!
Thy God has made of thee a greater man
Then Isten e'er of Magyar king or priest.

   CURTAIN.

ACT IV.

I. SCENE.

St. Sinbert's shrine. Inside. A chapel, occupying about one-half of the stage, whose front can be closed. Arnulf on the Catafalque. On each side three knights with torches or, three large candlesticks with lights, the knights presenting swords. Ulrich in the flowing dress of an abbot.

Ulrich [kneeling — then rising].
Let me alone with Arnulf's lifeless form.
Retire within the monastery walls
Until, perchance, my call shall summon you.
                              [*Exeunt in the rear.*]
[ULRICH *kneeling in a retired spot. Chapel doors close.*]

SCENE II. OUTSIDE THE CHAPEL.

[*Enter* LIUDOLF *with attendants.*]
At last Saint Sinbert's shrine beyond the walls.
I am the first, I see. Conrad and Arnulf
Still lag behind. [*To* ATTENDANTS]: Retire to your camp,
Alone will I expect my sworn allies. [*Exeunt.*]
The fates have been propitious to our cause.
Suabia is mine. Duke Conrad holds
Franconia's greater part. Bavaria

Has raised from end to end Count Arnulf's flag,
The Saxon chiefs are fettered by a truce
Which renders harmless their defeated corps.
The tribal dukes whose power the Emperor
Has vainly sought to crush beneath his heels
Raise everywhere their heads; their victory
Will be a victory for our cause.
If but to-night a final settlement
With Conrad and with Arnulf be arranged,
The hour of uncle Henry will have struck.
   [*Enters* CONRAD *alone.*]
Welcome, my brother Conrad — but alack,
Where is thy retinue?
 Conrad.   My royal prince,
Conrad no longer has a retinue;
He comes alone.
 Liudolf. What grim disaster robbed
My brother of his gallant following?
     Conrad.
'Twas no disaster, but my own free will,
I came this ev'n to you to plead for peace.
     Liudolf.
To plead for peace? A part most strange to play
For warlike Conrad. And 'twixt whom, I pray?

Conrad.
Between the father and the erring son.
Liudolf.
Marvel of marvels! lo, the insolent,
Proud, fire-eating Conrad of Lorraine
Has turned to bearer of the olive branch!
Of all the sights I saw the most grotesque!
Conrad.
'Tis passing strange, I grant. For proud I was —
Am still, perhaps — and poured my vial of wrath
And scathing scorn o'er saintly Ulrich's head.
Liudolf.
Aha! this change was worked by Ulrich's hand.
Conrad.
By Ulrich too, but not by him alone.
The wicked counsel which I offered thee
At Mainz; the more than half consent
I gave with fell result at Kudai's cave,
Began to smite my conscience to the quick
When I beheld fair Christian provinces
Trampled beneath the hoofs of Magyar horse.
New pangs convulsed me when my loved wife
Luitgard, Editha's and thy father's child,
Thy sister, Liudolf, died in my arms,

Her pleading, sobs and tears, her dying words
Brought Sinai's warning echoes back to me.
    Liudolf [*mockingly*].
A tale most touching, Duke, replete with
 tears ;
A dying sister robs a living brother
Of his ally, the strongest one he had —
Most touching, ay, for thee, but not for me.
And where comes in, my dear, this Augsburg
 Saint ?
    Conrad.
At Rhinlingen I lay with heavy heart
Confronted by your uncle Bruno's force,
When bishop Ulrich's visit to my tent —
What need of further talk ? — His fiery words,
Crushed as I was beneath the heavy blow,
Completely broke the ice. I made a truce,
And pledged myself to unconditional
Surrender to the King. I forthwith sent
Defiance to Lehel, the Magyar duke,
Who drank the mingled blood. At Langenzell
I paid my homage at your father's feet,
And there great Otto gave me his embrace.
    Liudolf.
And your fair duchy of Lorraine, no doubt ?
    Conrad.
Archbishop Bruno holds it for the time.

Liudolf [*bitterly*].
O Conrad, Conrad, thus thou keep'st thy word!
Now up in arms, now creeping in the dust;
Now fire and flame, and now a penitent!
What then, peacemaker, dost thou want of
  me? —
Go straightway to my father, humbly crouch,
My mouth full of submission, at his feet?
And what the outcome? — Dearest Liudolf,
Thou hast my pardon! But Suabia?
That goes to Burchard — uncle, well you know,
Of Adelheid! And whose the Roman crown?
'Twill to a marvel fit young Henry's brow.
No, Conrad, never! go your chosen way,
And I'll go mine.
    Conrad.   But listen, Liudolf,
'Twas I, may God forgive me, who misled
Thy ardent soul, thy high ambitious will,
Thy love of 'venture. Prince, dear brother,
  friend!
Grant me the only comfort which I crave,
Of yet undoing portion of the harm
I wickedly inflicted on thy soul.
    Liudolf.
Nay, nay, my soul to me. Your lack of pride,
Your tameness under smart of injury
Fit not my hate 'gainst Uncle Henry till

My heel is firmly planted on his breast.
And if my father still should choose to stand
Twixt him and me — well, let him share his
    fate.
     Conrad.
O curb, O curb, thy passion, Liudolf,
Thy morbid fancy and distorted will
Beneath God's fourth commandment.
 Liudolf.   Off with thee !
     Conrad.
I never knelt to mortal save my liege,
But now, I humbly bend my knee to thee,
Dear Liudolf, to pray thee to return —
     Liudolf.
Dear me no dear, apostate to the cause
Of ducal freedom. Up thou whining cur !
I spurn thee henceforth as a renegade.
  Conrad [*rising, in a changed, cold tone*].
Farewell, my prince, I harbor still the hope
Of one day fighting at your royal side
Against the infidels, whom I and you
Have summoned into our fatherland. [*Exit.*]
     Liudolf.
One prop is gone. The more must I rely
Upon myself. Arnulf, at least, is true ;
He'll not betray his friend, his brother now.
Why does he tarry ? Lo ! there is a light

Within St. Sinbert's lonely shrine. I might
As well retreat beneath its sheltering roof
Until the clarion notes of Arnulf's host
Announce the coming of my only friend.
                                    [*Chapel opens.*]

SCENE III. INSIDE OF THE CHAPEL. ULRICH KNEELING, UNOBSERVED BY LIUDOLF.

                  Liudolf.

A corpse, some knight, perhaps, of Ulrich's House.
[*Kneels down, rises again.*] I cannot pray, the walls repel my thoughts,
The saints frown darkly from their pedestals
Upon a cold intruder; pious words
Sound like a solemn mockery on my lips.
Give me an axe, an hour's battle toil
To lay that haunting ghost of Absalom,
King David's rebel dangling from the tree,
Whom Ulrich's magic art has conjured up
Before my troubled soul.
                Ulrich [*rises*].
                        Perhaps the sight of death
Will waken holier thoughts — thoughts of the past.
                  Liudolf.
I'm not alone! What meanest thou, good monk?

Ulrich.
Your purposed meeting at St. Sinbert's shrine
Beyond the wall is yet but half complete.
Liudolf.
Who told you, saint or devil, of the tryst?
Who placed upon your lips such croaking words
Of ominous intent?   [*Approaches the bier.*]
                    What's this? a grinning fright,
Or is it Arnulf? Nay, by heaven or hell
It cannot be! Say, Arnulf, is it thou?
He's still as death.   [*Shakes the corpse.*]
Rouse thee, my Arnulf! rise! [*Staggering back.*]
'Tis Arnulf — dead! my last support, my hope,
My only prop!   [*to* ULRICH, *coming closer.*]
            Hush, monk, I cannot pray,
My soul lies crushed beneath this leaden
    weight.   [*After a pause, calmer.*]
How came he by his death?
  Ulrich.   There was a war,
A bloody, impious, sacrilegious war,
Two sons against their sires, two Absaloms.
Liudolf.
Monk, demon, can you naught but rack my soul!
Beware, before you rouse a desperate!
  Ulrich [*throwing back his hood and mantle*].
Since when has Liudolf unlearned the prayers
He kneeling said at holy Edith's feet?

Liudolf.
Ulrich of Augsburg! My discomforture
Is now complete.
 Ulrich.   Thank God, my Liudolf,
That thou hast fallen into Ulrich's hand,
Who never ceased to yearn for his lost child.
E'en now, I need but give a signal and
St. Afra's war-worn veterans would seize
The felon and the rebel under ban.
But you have not to deal with liege and lord,
But with a father's sympathizing heart.
 Liudolf [*with apathy*].   Proceed.
 Ulrich. A father had two sons. The prodigal
Asked for his heir-loom, left his home and
 spent
His fortune rioting. Dost hear, my son?
    Liudolf.
His fortune rioting. I hear, proceed!
    Ulrich.
He spent his all, and soon began to feel,
Abandoned by his friends, the pangs of want.
Where are thy friends? Their shouts for
 Liudolf,
Their flying banners and their serried ranks?
Dost follow me?
    Liudolf.
Their serried ranks. I follow thee, proceed.

Ulrich.
Then said the prodigal: I'll rise at once,
And going to my father, plead with him.
I've sinned 'gainst heaven and against thyself,
I am not worthy now to be thy son;
O make me but a liegeman in thy house.
Liudolf.
Yea, make me but a liegeman in thy house.
Ulrich.
God, thy true Father, has been good to thee.
'Twas he who wrought the change in Conrad's soul;
A sign for thee! There lies Count Arnulf biered.
Another sign, vouchsafed to thee by him,
Who makes, rewards, avenges his command.
Liudolf [*suddenly roused*].
Stop, bishop, words will never clear this gloom.
My soul is torn by two conflicting storms:
The loss of Conrad and this shrouded bier,
And something in my soul — a haunting ghost,
Point up to Him, whose wrath is unappeased.
To sheath my sword, dismiss my followers,
Unbind their oaths, is but a play of boys;
But *now* to cower at my father's feet,

But *now* to shake my uncle Henry's hand,
But *now* to clasp the son of Adelheid
Unto my bosom, Arnulf on the bier,
Conrad a looker-on and Liudolf
Shorn of his power — nay, it cannot be.
   Ulrich.
Oh, give not way to vain delay of pride.
   Liudolf.
My crushed soul feels keenly, thy appeal.
But now, it cannot be! it cannot be!
I cannot rise and go — just now — no, hold
Your peace, dear father; rise and go I may;
But let me choose my time, my place, my terms.
   Ulrich.
Go now! 'tis terrible to play with God.
   Liudolf.
I fell as prince, as prince I will arise,
This much I promise thee, nor sword of mine
Nor hand of follower will ever more
Be raised against my father or his cause.
One question, holy bishop, where, oh, where,
Is Arnulf's soul?
 Ulrich.   Fear not for Arnulf's soul
Through my poor means the Savior's mercy chose
To save the soul of his repentant son.

Liudolf.
Then here I lay my hand on Arnulf's breast,
And swear to God that I will fight my way
Back to my father's heart, but mine the way.
First Liudolf must conquor Liudolf,
Meanwhile the son and prince will disappear.

CURTAIN

ACT V.

SCENE I. FOREST NEAR AUGSBURG.

Geysa.
The eventful day has come, that will decide
The fate of Geysa, and O, would to God
Of future Hungary. Before the sun
Has sunk behind the Lech — or Ulrich's God
Or Isten — shame, O Geysa, shame!
To join in single breath the true and false,
The God of peace with him of blood and war.
[*Looks around.*] My father tarries long, has he received
My token yet?
[*Enter* TOCSONY.]
Thy token I received,
And here I am.
Geysa. Welcome, my father dear.
The day has dawned. Oh, couldst thou not for once
Leave in thy leaders' hands this battle's fate?
Tocsony.
No, Geysa, cowardice is not my vice.
There stretch for miles the guarded wagon tents
Of Arpad's tribe, 100,000 steeds

Are neighing for the fray. There formed in ranks
Great Otto's arms are gleaming in the dawn;
The host is small but every man a man.
Here, on the Lechfield, soon the battle ground
Of two great nations, is Tocsony's place
To conquer with my tribesmen or to die.

Geysa.

But know you not, my father, wicked hands
Whose daggers threatened Geysa's harmless head,
Would gladly plunge them in my father's heart?

Tocsony.

The risk is slight. The disaffected crowd,
Led by Fynn-Ugria and Lehel, is small.
The nation, on the whole, stands true to me.

Geysa.

And, father, what the outcome of this day?

Tocsony.

To you alone, my son, I will reveal
My heart's presentiment. E'er from the day
This Otto's father, Saxon Henry, slew
At Merseburg, the flower of our race,
Disasters have o'ertaken our arms.
To-day, I know, are thousands of my men
Cowed by a hidden dread of that unarmed,
Mysterious priest, who proved to you, my son,
A father, but a terror to my folk.

Geysa.

Unhappy Geysa, placed between two fates!
If Otto conquers, Geysa's heart will bleed
For thee, my father dear! If our race
Shall win the bloody day, what will become
Of Ulrich, second father, and my trust
In Ulrich's God? Avaunt, foul, impious
  thought!
True God of heaven whatever be thy name,
Forgive my doubts! Into thy hands I lay
The issue of this day, my father's lot.
                [*A signal blast from the R.*]
The signal calls me back. Oh, fare thee well.
[*Embrace. Exeunt on opposite sides. Short
  march. Enter* OTTO, ULRICH, HENRY, CONRAD, MANGOLD, KNIGHTS, *etc.*]

Mangold.

'Twill be a fiery day. The Magyar odds
Are more than five to one against our force.
Like locust swarms their wiry cavalry
Is scouring o'er the plain.
   Ulrich.   With us is God.
                Otto.
And Ulrich's hand uplift.
   Henry.   And Conrad's arm.
          [HENRY *and* CONRAD *shake hands.*]

Conrad.
And former foes united round their king —
Old feuds forgotten, brotherhood restored.
Otto.
My heart beats high with hope when I behold
The champions of so many a field surround
St. Michael's standard, joined in one array.
But, O my Liubolf, my shattered hope,
Why art thou adsent on this day of days,
This battle of the Cross against its foes?
Ulrich.
There is still hope for him, my gracious liege,
I humbly trust that in his own good time
God's love will stand revealed in Liudolf.
[*Enters* KUNO.]
To arms, the Magyars fly their signal darts!
Otto.
Then forward, gentlemen, with God — I trust
To victory!
[*Exeunt R. Behind the scene L. the voice of* FYNN-UGRIA]: Onward to Isten's feast!
Lehel [*behind the scene L.*].
Throw to the vultures our foemen's skulls,
Bold Magyars.
Magyars [*behind the scene*].
Hooy, hooy, Magyar!

Henry of Bavaria [*behind the scene R.*].
With God and with St. Michael, forward men,
For home and Christendom!

Christian army [*behind the scene R.*].
For home and Christendom!

CURTAIN.

SCENE II. THE BATTLE ON THE LECHFELD —
TABLEAU.

In the tableau the R. of the stage is given to the Christian host, the L. to the Magyars. Otto I. occupies the middle front of the Christian group; to the right of him is Ulrich, holding a crucifix aloft. Still further to the right of Otto, Conrad forms the center of a group. To the left of Otto, towards the foreground of the stage, the black knight pierces a Magyar who is attacking Otto. On the L. of stage, Tocsony in center, to his left Fynn-Ugria, to his right Lehel. In the background Magyars turning or fleeing.

CURTAIN.

SCENE III. OPEN PLACE IN FOREST.

Lehel.

Here, quick, look sharp; they are at our heels.
The day is lost, our tens of thousands slain
And Arpad's children scattered to the winds.
One thing remains to do.

Toltan.   To save our chief.

Lehel.

Tocsony? Give his carcass to the crows,
Revenge is our work. Some desperate men
Prepared to face, unmoved the jaws of death
May still convulse this realm and Christendom.

Fynn-Ugria.

I am the man!

[*Others*]: And I, and I, and we.

Fynn-Ugria.

This day of woe I'm cured of hope and life;
Revenge, revenge, the last dim ray of joy!

Lehel.

Then scattering among the underbrush
Await the signal blast of Arpad's horn,
Its sound will tell you where to make a rush
And send your poisoned darts and javelins.
Thus Otto, Ulrich, Conrad and their staff,
May still become the prey of Arpad's race,
If we but know to die.

84   *Liudolf.*

Fynn-Ugria.   To die we know.
                    Lehel.
The rest ye leave to me. One quest I crave:
Revenge on Conrad of the reddish hair
Be mine. He broke the covenant of blood.
Into my teeth defiance bold he hurled,
Drew off his perjured friends from our side
And turned his traitorous sword against our race,
Duke Conrad must be touched by none but me.
                    All.
Agreed.
Lehel.   Then hie ye to your ambuscade.
                              [*Exeunt.*]
     [*Enter* OTTO, MANGOLD, CONRAD.]
                    Otto.
Oh, for a cup of water!   [*Exit* MANGOLD.]
                              My parched tongue
Is cleaving to my mouth.
                    Conrad.
                              No German eye
Has ever seen a day like this.
[MANGOLD *returns with a helmet full of water and offers it to the* EMPEROR.]
     Otto.   First ye,
I do command, the rest for me. [*Drinks.*] My thanks —
To God the King of kings, my humble praise.

Mangold.
God struck the foe and, striking, used the arm
Of our Otto.
  Otto.   Hush, good Mangold, hush;
Three champions I looked upon to-day
Such as our century will not produce
A second time. High on his mettled horse
Sat Ulrich, bare of steeled mail or shield,
Untouched by spear or flying javelin,
Holding aloft the sacred crucifix.
Then there was Conrad, our gallant Duke.
     Conrad.
Nay, gracious liege, I was but one of them;
There were four Conrads in the thick of fight.
     Otto.
Peace, Conrad! East and west and north and south
I saw thy cleaving broadsword fell the foe.
And still a third — who knows his crest or name?
Black as a thunder cloud, as lighting swift,
Strong as a northern blast. He swept his sword
All round and round, a mowing scythe of death,
And in the hottest fray my life he saved.
Seek me at once the hero knight in black.

[*Outside a blast of Arpad's horns and cries of
"Hooy, hooy, Magyar!"*]

Mangold.

A Magyar ambush!

Conrad.

Up, to arms! To arms!

[*Enter* ULRICH, GEYSA *and* ATTENDANTS.]

Ulrich.

Stay undisturbed, my gracious majesty.
The knight in black had sharper eyes and fangs
Than Magyar craft. They're in full flight by this.

[*Behind the scene* HENRY'S *voice.*]

Turn, heathen cowards, stabbing in the back —
Turn round and show your face. Bavarians,
Pursue the treacherous hounds and bring them here.

Geysa [*kneeling to* ULRICH].

O, father mine, and savior of my life,
To-day thy God has conquered Isten's realm.
I trembling bow to him in awe and love.
Yon flows a sparkling fount, what hinders thee
Baptizing Geysa who believes thy faith!

Ulrich.

With joyful heart I grant thy holy wish.

Otto.

The let me be godfather to this boy,
Geysa, first Christian prince of Magyar blood.

Ulrich.

Come, follow me.

[*Exeunt R. Enter L.* HENRY *of* BAVARIA, AT-
TENDANTS, LEHEL, FINN-UGRIA, *etc., bound.*]

Henry of Bavaria.

We've caught the treacherous band,
Trying by murderous snare to turn the tide
Of this eventful day. The gallows be
The doom deserved by these mere highway-
men.

Mangold.

Wait, noble duke, and let the Emperor
Decide their fate.

[*Enter* OTTO, ULRICH, GEYSA *in white.*]

Otto.

Whom have we here?

Henry.

Conspirators, who sought
To gain by murder what they lost in fight.

Otto.

What say'st thou, Magyar prince, in thy defense?

Lehel.

The Magyars are abandoned by their gods,
Because their war god Isten was betrayed
By one of Arpad's blood [*points to* GEYSA].

Otto.   Do not blaspheme,
It was the one true God who won the day.

Fynn-Ugria.
To chide the fallen is the conqueror's right.
Lehel.
I own defeat. The Lechfeld is the tomb
Of all the bravest of a conquered race.
Be't so. But yet it cuts me to the quick
To see that Conrad sitting as my judge.
'Twas he who lured us to this ill-starred land.
Henry of Bavaria.
You never heard of Christian penitence.
To fall is human, but to rise divine.
Conrad [*kneeling to* OTTO].
A boon, victorious liege, a boon to-day,
The life of this undaunted Magyar chief!
Lehel.
Nay, King and Duke, I spurn your mocking boon
Return to me but Arpad's battle horn,
My faithful and inseparable friend,
To sound the death song of my fallen race.
I lost the horn beneath my wounded horse.
Kuno [*steps forward*].
I found this battle horn among the slain.
Otto.
Then free his hands and let him sound his lay.

Lehel.
[*Blows, and, approaching* CONRAD, *draws his hidden dagger and stabs him.*]
Thou shalt precede me, thou shalt be my slave
In Isten's realm.
Conrad.
An evil deed once wooed will work its end.
'Twas I who led poor Liudolf astray.
Thy words were true, O Ulrich, I accept
This blow as just atonement for my sins
Against the Fourth Commandment. O my liege,
O, father of my wife, forgive thy son.
Otto.
I have forgiven thee.
Ulrich. Dost thou forgive
The hand that struck thee down?
Conrad. I do, I do.
Ulrich.
Then cleansed by grace divine and penance stern,
O soul of Conrad, rise through Christ to God.
[*Conrad dies.*]
Otto.
St. Michael's standard be the hero's shroud.
Rupert [*behind the scene L.*].
Another prize!

Eberhard [*behind the scene L.*].
                    The greatest yet of all.
This time a true blue-blooded Arpadeer!
[*Enter soldiers with* TOCSONY *from L.* GEYSA
quickly walks over to his father.]
                Geysa.
My father, I am now thy Christian son,
Baptized by Ulrich's hand.
  Tocsony.   Thy God
To-day proved stonger than the Magyar gods.
                Geysa.
And if we should return to Hungary
Wilt thou allow the practice of my faith?
  Tocsony.   I will.
          Geysa [*to* OTTO].
            Then, Otto, conquering king,
From thee, my Christian sponsor, do I ask
My father's life and liberty.
  Otto.   Not life alone,
But all his kingdom shall remain to him,
On certain terms to be agreed upon,
And shall devolve on thee at his demise.
And may a Christian king one happy day
Unite the Magyar tribes with Christendom.
          [*To* TOCSONY, *pointing to* GEYSA.]
O happy father, blessed with such a son!

When shall my prodigal, my Liudolf,
Long lost, alas, long dead to me, return
Unto his father's heart, and coming fill
The aching void which Edith's first-born son
Alone can fill.

[*Outside, song as in Act II. and shouts!* " *The* KNIGHT IN BLACK, *hurrah, the* SABLE KNIGHT!" *Enter* LIUDOLF, *the* KNIGHT IN BLACK, *and* SOLDIERS].

Otto.

Ha, welcome hero of the battle field,
Quick, bravest of the brave, thy name, thy house.
Down with thy visor, show thy manly face,
To you, to you, I owe my limbs and life.

Ulrich.

Thou helper, heaven-sent in sore distress,
Reveal thy face.

[LIUDOLF *uncovers his face and kneels with outstretched arms before his father.*]

Thanks, heaven, 'tis he, 'tis he!

Otto [*lifting up* LIUDOLF *and embracing him.*]
My son! my son! up to thy father's heart!

Ulrich.

Atonement just and restoration sweet,

And holy sanction and reward here meet:
And Thee we hail, with uplift heart and hand,
Eternal Guardian of the Fourth Command.

CURTAIN.

THE END.

www.ingramcontent.com/pod-product-compliance
Lightning Source LLC
Chambersburg PA
CBHW020259090426
42735CB00009B/1143